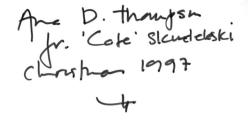

SMITH & HAWKEN

BOOK *of* DAYS

THE

PERENNIAL

COMPANION

WORKMAN PUBLISHING

NEW YORK

Workman Publishing Company
708 Broadway
New York, NY 10003-9555

Manufactured by Arnoldo Mondadori, Verona, Italy

First printing, August 1997
10 9 8 7 6 5 4 3 2 1

ISBN 0-7611-0832-7

"What a delight it is,
When, of a morning,
I get up and go out
To find in full bloom a flower
That yesterday was not there."

—TACHIBANA AKEMI

JANUARY

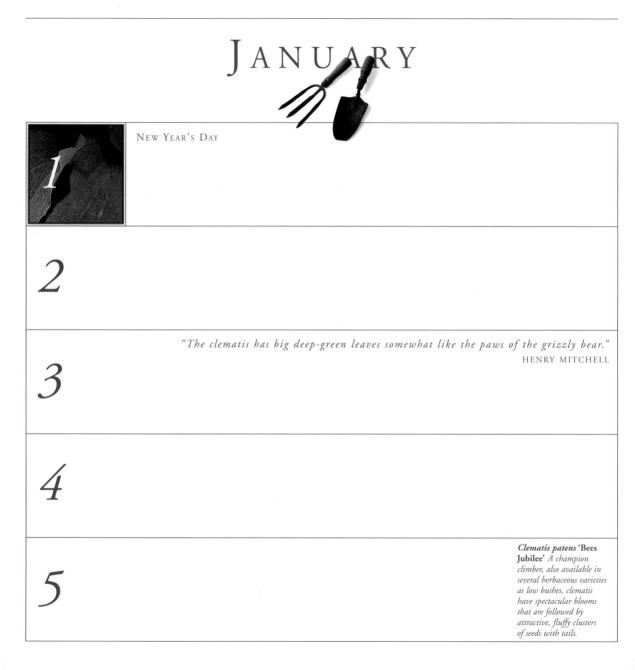

1 NEW YEAR'S DAY

2

"The clematis has big deep-green leaves somewhat like the paws of the grizzly bear."
HENRY MITCHELL

3

4

5

Clematis patens '**Bees Jubilee**' *A champion climber, also available in several herbaceous varieties as low bushes, clematis have spectacular blooms that are followed by attractive, fluffy clusters of seeds with tails.*

6

7

Tulips, Hyacinths,
and **Aubrietas**
A fragrant reward for preparations made the previous fall, this rock garden is awash with spring-blooming bulbs (tulips and hyacinths) and shocking pink aubrietas.

J A N U A R Y

8

9

"A garden I tend whose blossoms never existed." PABLO NERUDA

10

11

12

13

14

15

MARTIN LUTHER KING JR.'S BIRTHDAY

16

17

18

19

Rudbeckia fulgida **'Goldsturm'** *and* **Salvia farinacea** *These golden-yellow coneflowers will bloom from midsummer through fall and make excellent companions to the whorled spikes of the mealy-cup sage.*

JANUARY

20

21

22

JANUARY

23

24

25

Crocus vernus These
Dutch crocuses create a
carpet of extra-large,
chalice-shaped flowers
in mid spring. They will
thrive and naturalize
even in lawns.

26

27

"A woman tries to comfort me. She puts her hand under my shirt and writes the names of flowers on my back." MARK STRAND

28

29

30

Aquilegia **'Dorothy'**
Fondly known as columbine, aquilegias have a fairylike woodland quality with gracefully posed flowers and lacy green foliage appearing in early summer.

31

FEBRUARY

1

2

3

"The blossoms are so short, the forgetting so long." WALT WHITMAN

4

5

Alcea rosea *An old-fashioned beauty, the hollyhock best resides against a fence or wall or holding court at the back of an herbaceous border. Older varieties reach up to 9 feet.*

6

7

"...all is permitted the rose-splendor, a conspiracy of perfumes, petalous flesh that tempts the nose, the lips, the teeth." COLETTE

8

9

10

11

Allium, Fennel, Purple Sage, *and* **Lavender**
In this fragrant green and purple-pink border, the allium's magenta puff-balls mingle with florets of lavender—a color echoed by the leaves of the purple sage.

12

13

14

VALENTINE'S DAY

15

16

17

"The peony has the privilege of putting us in touch with the true spring." COLETTE

18

19

20

Paeonia mlokosewitschii
A dollop of lemon chiffon, this cold-loving peony is easily grown in sun or partial shade, and enjoys a brief flowering in April or early May.

FEBRUARY

Rosa **'Constance Spry'**
*A David Austin rose,
'Constance Spry' is the
first modern shrub rose
(1961) to offer all the
charm, fullness, rich color,
and myrrh fragrance of
the old-fashioned classics.*

21

22

WASHINGTON'S BIRTHDAY

23

24

25

26

27

"I perhaps owe having become a painter to flowers." CLAUDE MONET

28

29

MARCH

1

"Spring unlocks the flowers to paint the laughing soil." REGINALD HEBER

2

3

4

5

*Erythronium tuolum-
nense, Anemone blanda*
Known variously as fawn
lily, adder's tongue, and
alpine lily, erythroniums
thrive in shade and partial
shade, growing almost
twice as tall (12 to 15
inches) as these anemones.

MARCH

6

7

8

"The delicate droop of the petals standing out in relief is like the eyelid of a child."
AUGUSTE RODIN

9

10

11

MARCH

Geranium × *magnificum*
In late spring and early summer, this geranium bears blue-veined, violet-hued flowers, and continues to show color in fall with vivid red and burnt-orange foliage.

12

13

MARCH

14

15

16

17 ST. PATRICK'S DAY

18

19

Rosa **'Elizabeth of Glamis'** *Bearing very fragrant double flowers the color of melon flesh, this rose, like all floribundas, produces generous clusters of blooms on a vigorous bush—offering a bouquet with each cut.*

MARCH

20

"*Deep in their roots, all flowers keep the light.*" THEODORE ROETHKE

21

22

MARCH

23

24

25

**Columbine, Lamb's
Ears, Roses** *In this floral
fairyland thicket, the
columbine blossoms appear
as exotic winged creatures,
darting in and among the
silvery lamb's ears, and
pausing to smell the
occasional pink rose.*

26

27

28

"There seems to be so much more winter than we need this year." KATHLEEN NORRIS

29

30

31

Zantedeschia aethiopica
A favorite image of Art Deco artists, the creamy calla lily—whether tightly furled like a scroll or fully blown—lends a sculptural beauty to the spring and early summer garden.

April

1

2

3

4

5

APRIL

6

7

Paeonia 'Sarah
Bernhardt' *Herbaceous
peonies need to experience
a solid winter chill to
proffer the floriferous,
cabbagelike blooms that
make them one of the
garden's undisputed stars.*

8

9

10

"Maybe rosebud was something he couldn't get or something he lost." ORSON WELLES

11

12

13

Chionodoxa gigantea luciliae *Called glory-of-the-snow, these starry, alpine meadow natives are among the first bulbs to bloom in spring and will self-sow freely in hospitable conditions.*

14

15

16

"A garden really lives only insofar as it is an expression of faith, the embodiment of a hope and a song of praise." RUSSELL PAGE

17

18

19

20

21

Tulipa 'Princess Irene' and **Myosotis** *Waking up the spring garden, hot orange tulips rise up like flames from the cool violet mass of forget-me-nots—a combination that is equally arresting in the vase.*

22

23

24

"Remember that the most beautiful things in the world are the most useless;
peacocks and lilies for instance." JOHN RUSKIN

25

26

27

APRIL

28

Hemerocallis **'Sing Mara'**
*Although each spectacular
flower lasts only one day
(hence the common name,
daylily), this plant is
extremely prolific, making
it a natural for any
perennial or shrub border.*

29

30

MAY

1

2

"Chrysanthemums...smell of moths, camphorball and drowned sailors." SIR ROBERT SITWELL

3

4

5

Meconopsis grandis
A difficult-to-grow relative of the poppy, this rare, shade-loving plant bears flowers with peacock-blue petals that contrast beautifully with its surrounding green foliage.

6

7

**Osteospermum
'Buttermilk'** *A type of
African daisy, these pale
yellow sun worshippers
are in their element when
gathered in fat bunches
and displayed in a milk
jug, water pitcher, or
galvanized flower bucket.*

MAY

8

9

10

"Each plant is a personality, each kind of herb a fragrant memory." ROSETTA CLARKSON

11

12

13

14

15

16

"John says he never cares about the flowers of 'em, but men have no eye for anything neat. He says his favorite flower is a cauliflower." THOMAS HARDY

17

18

Rugosa Roses
These modern shrub roses make excellent hedges, and many offer a bonus of autumn color and hips in addition to masses of clustered blooms.

19

MAY

20

21

"In joy or sadness, flowers are our constant friends. We eat, drink, sing, dance, and flirt with them." KOKUZO OKAKURA

22

MAY

23

Narcissus 'Hawera' *and*
Myosotis 'Dwarf Indigo'
In nature as in life,
opposites attract; the
intense golden-yellow of
the daffodil trumpets
turns up the volume on
the tiny purple clusters
of forget-me-nots.

24

25

26

27

28

29

TRADITIONAL MEMORIAL DAY

30

31

*Aquilegia × **hybrida***
Poised like some exotic species of dragonfly caught in mid-flight, this fiery member of the columbine family is also attractive to hummingbirds, who fancy its nectar-filled spurs.

JUNE

1

2

3

"By planting flowers one invites butterflies." CHAO CH'ANG

4

5

JUNE

6

7

Freesia 'Royal Mixed'
This motley of fragrant blooming flowers creates a carnival of color in the garden. Potted up in a container, freesias are easier to grow and less susceptible to disease.

8

9

10

"No two gardens are the same. No two days are the same in one garden." HUGH JOHNSON

11

12

13

Phlox paniculata 'Windsor' *The sweetly fragrant, silky-soft flower heads of summer phlox are attractive to birds as well as to people, and make an excellent filler for the middle or back of a sunny border.*

14

15

16

17

18

Platycodon grandiflorus
This charming, clump-forming summer bloomer is also known as balloon-flower because of the shape of its buds before they unfurl into violet stars.

19

20

21

22

23

24 ST. JEAN BAPTISTE DAY (CANADA)

25

"In the spring, at the end of the day, you should smell like dirt." MARGARET ATWOOD

26

27

JUNE

28

29

30

Roses, Loosestrife, Catmint, *and* Geraniums
Within this classic cottage garden roses consort with violet-blue flowers of Geranium magnificum, *clump-forming spires of* Lysimachia punctata, *and silvery* Nepata.

JULY

1 CANADA DAY (CANADA)

2

3

4 INDEPENDENCE DAY

5

Colchicum speciosum
Sometimes called autumn crocuses, these pink, crown-shaped flowers are harbingers of cooler weather, appearing in the garden long after the true crocuses have faded from view.

6

7

Helleborus orientalis
'White Swan' *One of the
loveliest of the shade-loving
perennials, hellebores have
extended blooming times
(two to three months) and
shiny, deeply divided evergreen foliage that provides
interest all winter.*

8

9

10

"One could not pluck a flower without troubling a star." FRANCIS THOMPSON

11

12

13

14

15

16

*"People from a planet without flowers would think we must be mad with joy…
to have such things about us."* IRIS MURDOCH

17

18

19

***Lavandula* spp.**
*The flowing rows of
lavender in this knot
garden impart a wave-
like feeling when a gentle
breeze sweeps over them.
Their rich purple foliage
almost necessitates
massing them together.*

JULY

20

"...In the garden, after a rainfall, you can faintly, yes, hear the breaking of new blooms."
TRUMAN CAPOTE

21

22

JULY

Tulips *and* Pansies
A sunset-hued border is painted with fiery tulips that rise like tongues of flame from the velvety, blood-red pansies, Viola × wittrockiana, *which are also known as heartsease.*

23

24

25

26

27

28

"Flowers leave some of their fragrance in the hand that bestows them." CHINESE PROVERB

29

30

31

Hydrangea macrophylla **'Nikko Blue'** *A cooling note to the summer garden, blue-purple hydrangeas benefit from an application of aluminum sulfate to the soil (which keeps the flowers from emerging pink).*

AUGUST

1

2

3

"Flowers really do intoxicate me." VITA SACKVILLE-WEST

4

5

***Crinum* × *powellii*
'Alba'** *Shaped like a lily,
and similarly fragrant,
crinums are available
in both red and white
cultivars.*

6

7

8

"Each flower is a soul opening out to nature." GERARD DE NERVAL

9

10

11

AUGUST

Rosa 'Ausblush'
*These shrub roses are
amass with cupped,
fully double flowers
whose pale pink-tissue
petals are set off by glossy
dark green foliage.*

12

13

14

15

"Here comes the time when, vibrating on its stem, every flower fumes like a censer; noises and perfumes circle in the evening air." CHARLES BAUDELAIRE

16

17

18

19

Erigeron '**Dignity**' *and* **Erigeron** '**Försters Liebling**' *Close relatives of the Michaelmas daisy, these early summer-to-fall bloomers have golden centers framed by frills of hot pink and cool lavender.*

AUGUST

20

"To me the meanest flower that blows can give thoughts that do often lie too deep for tears."
WILLIAM WORDSWORTH

21

22

AUGUST

23

24

25

Allium giganteum The giant of the ornamental onions, this allium stands 35 to 45 inches tall, and its purple, globe-shaped flower heads create visual interest on many levels.

26

27

28

"Earth laughs in flowers." RALPH WALDO EMERSON

29

30

31

Rosa 'Altissimo' *This modern climber proffers very large single flowers in bright carmine red, a color heightened by the glossy, dark green foliage.*

SEPTEMBER

1	
2	
3	
4	
5	

SEPTEMBER

6

7

Kniphofia rooperi
*Emerging from clumps
of grasslike leaves that
resemble tiki torches,
these robust marshland
natives—also known as
red-hot pokers—are a
beacon for hummingbirds.*

8

9

10

"The love of flowers is really the best teacher of how to grow and understand them." MAX SCHLING

11

12

13

Parrot Tulips *and* **Forget-Me-Nots** *Striped a candy-cane pink and white—with a splash of green—these frilled, spring-blooming parrot tulips rise up through a froth of forget-me-nots (Myosotis 'Dwarf Indigo').*

14

15

16

17

18

19

20

21

Aquilegia flabellata
*The petals of this delicate,
downward-facing columbine
resemble swans meeting in
the center of a pond. For a
second crop of snowy white
flowers, cut back old stems.*

22

23

24

"Neither the flower nor its influence can be explained." COLETTE

25

26

27

S E P T E M B E R

28

29

30

Omphalodes cappadocica *Growing in the wild on shady rocks and cliffs and along forest streams, this creeping evergreen is best protected from hard frosts.*

OCTOBER

1

2

"All gardeners know better than other gardeners." CHINESE PROVERB

3

4

5

Viola **'Penny Wood'**
A staple of English herb gardens for centuries (and a champion self-sower), this beloved perennial woodland violet flashes its purple-blue flowers in spring.

6

7

Dendranthema 'Brown Eyes' *and* **Aster amellus** 'Lady Hindlip'
The creamy orange, tightly packed pom-poms of the dendranthema (a close cousin of chrysanthemum) contrast with the purple spiked asters.

OCTOBER

8

9

"More things grow in the garden than the gardener sows." SPANISH PROVERB

10

11

12

TRADITIONAL COLUMBUS DAY

13

OCTOBER

14

15

16

17

18

19

Geranium 'Claridge Druce' *A showy, pink-flowering plant with a long blooming season, this geranium forms weed-proof clumps that are easily propagated by division.*

OCTOBER

20

21

"I guess a good gardener always starts as a good weeder." AMOS PETTINGILL

22

OCTOBER

Geraniums, Violets, Bellflowers, Lady's Mantle, *and* **Weigela**
Summer color is provided at all levels of this perennial border highlighted by Alchemilla mollis (lady's mantle) and the striking variegated weigela leaves.

23

24

25

26

27

28

29

30

31

HALLOWEEN

Rosa **'Louise Odier'**
*A stately old rose with
an intoxicating scent,
'Louise Odier' dates from
1851 and is still a strong
and robust bloomer,
unlike some of its
Bourbon cousins.*

November

1

2

"There are connoisseurs of blue just as there are lovers of wine." COLETTE

3

4

5

NOVEMBER

6

7

Delphinium, Sweet William, *and* **Roses**
In this rampant summer border, blue spires of delphiniums tower over the bicolored blossoms of Sweet William (Dianthus barbatus) *and intermingle with crimson clusters of roses.*

8

9

10

11

VETERANS DAY
REMEMBRANCE DAY (CANADA)

12

13

Lilium candidum The
Madonna lily scents the
evening garden with
a heady fragrance redolent
of sweet violets; it thrives
in soil that has been
enriched with calcium
or wood ashes.

14

15

16

"I left the big poppy, with its blue pollen and its slowly unfolding silk, to the fields and gardens. Long afterward, I came upon it again, in Paris, behind closed doors." COLETTE

17

18

19

20

21

Roses, Geraniums, *and* **Poppies** *In this tapestry of sugary pinks and violets, fat Oriental poppies—with their pale, crinkled silk blossoms—commune with a mass of fragrant roses and an underplanting of geraniums.*

© BRIGITTE THOMAS/GARDEN PICTURE LIBRARY

22

23

24

"There is nothing more pleasant than spading when the ground is soft and damp."
JOHN STEINBECK

25

26

27

NOVEMBER

Polygonatum odoratum **'Variegatum'** *Reliable in a shade garden, the white, bell-like flowers of Japanese variegated Solomon's seal appear in spring on pink-tinted stems, and exude a sweet, light fragrance in the evening.*

28

29

30

DECEMBER

1

2

"Rose is a rose is a rose." GERTRUDE STEIN

3

4

5

Rosa 'Glad Tidings'
A rose worthy of Carmen,
this intensely crimson
floribunda produces
masses of large clusters
of semi-double flowers set
off by glossy green foliage.

6

7

8

"The plant world is not mute, though the sound of its activity reaches us." COLETTE

9

10

11

DECEMBER

12

13

Helleborus foetidus
'Wester Flisk' *Panicles
of these nodding, rose-like,
apple-green flowers edged
with pink appear from
January through April.
They bloom for several
months in shade or
partial shade.*

14

15

"Flowers are restful to look at. They have neither emotions nor conflicts." SIGMUND FREUD

16

17

18

Rosa **'Raubritter'** *This bushy shrub rose produces masses of cupped, fully double, bubble-gum pink flowers along slender, arching branches—a spectacular sight when in full flush.*

19

DECEMBER

20

21

> *"What is a weed? A plant whose virtues have not yet been discovered."*
> RALPH WALDO EMERSON

22

DECEMBER

Dianthus **Highland Hybrids** *and* **Campanula persicifolia** *White and purple bells of campanula nod above a mass of clove-scented pinks. Each blossom is a willing boutonniere— perhaps worn to celebrate the return of spring.*

23

24

25

CHRISTMAS

26

DECEMBER

27

28

"Bread feeds the body indeed, but flowers feed also the soul." THE KORAN

29

30

31

Meconopsis grandis
Cultivated around shepherds' huts in Sikkim, where the seeds are used for oil, this shade lover produces flowers with bright blue, tissue-thin petals that catch the slightest breeze.

"*I cherish the mourning doves, the cardinals whistling farewell to the day, and the rare visitations of evening grosbeaks and bluebirds that make one feel, quite unjustifiably, like one of the chosen.*"

—Eleanor Perenyi

NOTES